rather*losangeles*

researched, photographed and written by amy blessing, annie campbell and anna h. blessing

toc

neighborhoods

EAT

angelini osteria
animal
axe
baby blues bbq
broome street general store
café de leche
canelé
church & state
daikokuya
el huarache azteca
eveleigh
food + lab
fugetsu-do
gjelina
gta (gjelina take away)
good girl dinette
grand central market
lamill coffee
lark cake shop
lindy & grundy
mendocino farms
mo-chica
mother dough
nickel diner
palate food + wine
pho café
salt's cure
scoops
shima
soot bull jeep
son of a gun
the lazy ox canteen
the tasting kitchen
valerie confections
viet noodle bar
wurstkuche

SHOP

aardvark letterpress
bar keeper
bazar
botany
bountiful
casbah café and bazaar
church
creatures of comfort
df feet
eggy
feal mor
french general
gibson
house on genesee
ige
iko iko
inheritance
jake·
kellygreen
lake
liz's antique hardware
lost and found stores
milkmade
mister freedom
mohawk general store /
amsterdam modern
mother plucker feather co.
new high (m)art
new stone age
noodle stories
obsolete
ok
ooga booga
plastica
post 26
reform school
rolling greens
rth
society of the spectacle
south willard
sugar paper
tavin
tenoversix
tortoise
tortoise general store
traveler's bookcase

notes
about
los angeles

rather *los angeles* EDITORS >

Amy Blessing is the co-owner of Apartment Number 9 with her sister Sarah, contributes to Design*Sponge as part of the BBB Craft Sisters and plans parties with her childhood friend Annie.

Annie Campbell is a food enthusiast with a catering and party design business in LA.

Anna H. Blessing is the author of more than a dozen *eatshop guides* as well as the upcoming book, "Locally Grown: Portraits of Artisanal Farms from America's Heartland." She is also one of the BBB Craft Sisters.

We love a good makeover, and Los Angeles is the perfect place for one. Anyone can become anything here, and finding yourself might mean a personal transformation that happens again and again and again. Transformation, evolution, metamorphosis—whatever you call it—it happens at lightspeed in this city, to both people and places—shops and restaurants most definitely included.

It's true that Tinseltown has plenty of glitz and glam, and some places even manage to live up to their media hype. But there are many more places that are below the radar, tucked away in lesser-known neighborhoods, oozing with authenticity. We hope you'll enjoy exploring the places we think make this city full of energy, creativity and lots of good eating and shopping.

Finally, if you find yourself in need of a some downtime from eating and shopping, here are some suggestions outside of that realm:

1 > Eames House: Walk around the exterior and peek through the windows to check out Charles and Ray's home in its original state.

2 > Hollywood Farmer's Market: Okay, so technically this is both eating and shopping, but compelling enough to also be sightseeing.

3 > Yoga at Golden Bridge: A physical and spiritual experience not to be missed if you really want a dose of L.A. living.

4 > Thai massage at Pho Siam: You're going to need this after the yoga. Make it a theme day and stop by Pho Café for a bowl of goodness afterward.

5 > The Getty Museum: Views, architecture and art at Richard Meier's glowing white structure.

it's all about...

exploring locally

*discovering a sense of place
behind the veneer of a city*

*experiencing what gives
a city its soul through its
local flavor*

rather EVOLUTION

If you are thinking that this book looks suspiciously like an *eat.shop guide*, you're on to something. As of October 2011, the *eat.shop guides* evolved into **rather** to give readers a more vibrant experience when it comes to local eating and shopping. It's all about what you'd **rather** be doing with your time when you explore a city—eat at a chain restaurant or an intimate little trattoria devouring dishes the chef created from farm fresh ingredients? You get the idea.

USING **rather**

All of the businesses featured in this book are first and foremost locally owned, and they are chosen to be featured because they are utterly authentic and uniquely conceived. And since this isn't an advertorial guide, there's no money exchanging hands • Make sure to double check the hours of the business before you go, as many places change their hours seasonally • The pictures and descriptions for each business are meant to give a feel for a place, but please know those items may no longer be available • Our maps are stylized, meaning they don't show every street • Small local businesses have always had to work that much harder to keep their heads above water, and not all the businesses featured will stay open. Please go to the **rather** website for updates • **rather** editors research, shoot and write everything you see in this book • Only natural light is used to shoot and there's no styling or propping

restaurants >
$ = inexpensive $$ = medium $$$ = expensive

Go to **rather.com** to learn more

where to lay your weary head

maison 140
140 lasky drive (beverly hills)
310.281.4000 / maison140beverlyhills.com
standard double from $150
restaurant: bar noir
notes: boutique hotel, kelly wearstler-style

the london
1020 north san vicente boulevard
(west hollywood)
866.282.4560 / thelondonwesthollywood.com
standard double from $249
restaurants: boxwood cafe, gordon ramsay
notes: big and beautiful with a rooftop pool

the farmer's daughter
115 south fairfax avenue (mid-city west)
800.334.1658 / farmersdaughterhotel.com
standard double from $155
restaurant: tart restaurant
notes: quirky, country-meets-city style motel

palihouse
8465 holloway drive (west hollywood)
323.656.4100 / palihouse.com
standard double from $200
restaurant: courtyard brasserie
notes: mod all-suite urban lodge

the ambrose
1255 20th street (santa monica)
310.315.1555 / ambrosehotel.com
standard double from $150
notes: holistic hospitality

for more hotel choices, visit >

losangeleshotel.net

TravelShark

PART OF THE TRAVELSHARK
TRAVEL NETWORK

more eating gems

*these businesses appeared in
previous editions of eat.shop los angeles*

EAT

3 square cafe
alcove cafe & bakery
alegria on sunset
auntie em's kitchen
beechwood
best fish taco in ensenada
blair's
bld
bluebird café
bob's coffee and donuts
cafe mimosa
cafe nagomi
cafe tropical
carmela ice cream
chameau
chez jay
clementine
colorado wine company
coolhaus
delilah bakery
dominick's
empanada's place
ford's filling station
gingergrass
graffeo
inaka
jin patisserie
joan's on third
la serenata de garibaldi
little next door
lou
loteria! grill
magnolia
malibu seafood
manpuku
mao's kitchen
mashti malone's
mexico city
milk
moishe's
musso & frank grill
nook bistro
pace

pacific dining car
port royal
reddi chick
samosa house and
bharat bazaar
silverlake wine
singapore's banana leaf
sona
square one dining
umami burger
the arsenal
the cheese store of
beverly hills
the cheese store of silverlake
the gumbo pot
the hungry cat
village idiot

more shopping gems

these businesses appeared in
previous editions of eat.shop los angeles

downtown

japantown

eat

shop

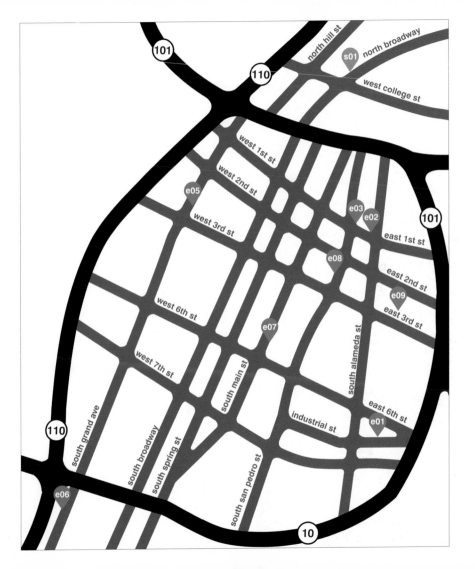

church & state

industrial chic bistro

1850 Industrial Street
Between Sixth and Seventh
(Downtown) *map E01*
213.405.1434
www.churchandstatebistro.com

twitter @churchstatela
see website for hours
lunch. dinner
$$-$$$ reservations recommended

Yes, Please: *ginger grape press, champagne cocktail, escargots de bourgogne, assiette de charcuterie, tarte flambée, omelette forestière, pot de crème au chocolat*

People often use geographical references to describe the places where they eat. For example, if a restaurant in Chicago reminds me of one that could be found in the Pacific Northwest city I grew up in, I call it Portland-y. Admit it, everybody plays this game because it helps to define the feel of a place. I found myself doing this with **Church & State**. It feels nothing like L.A. and much more like New York, or scratch that, a mix of New York and Paris. With its bistro atmosphere, well-researched French menu and a chef who's got the magic touch—I guess I should say that it feels most like Heaven.

daikokuya

ramen, ramen, ramen!

327 East First Street
Between San Pedro and Alameda
(Little Tokyo) *map E02*
213.626.1680
www.daikoku-ten.com

mon - thu 11a - midnight fri - sat 11a - 1a
sun 11a - 11p
lunch. dinner
$ first come, first served

Yes, Please: *oolong shochu, ramune soda, gyoza, tsukemono, sliced kurobuta pork belly, daikoku ramen, tsukemen ramen, shredded pork belly*

What is a ramenhead? It's a person who spits on the ground when the words "Top Ramen" are uttered. This someone also belongs to ramen chat rooms and endlessly discusses the best ramen spots in a city, what their soup bases are made out of and the texture of the noodles. Though I love the stuff, alas, I am no ramenhead. Unfortunately, the last ramen I ate tasted like a bowl of barnyard. Memorable, though not delicious. The ramen at **Daikokuya** is both—with its rich broth, slices of pork belly, chijuri-style egg noodles, and a marinated boiled egg bobbing about. Yum.

fugetsu-do

japanese confectionary and bakery

315 East First Street
Between San Pedro and Alameda
(Little Tokyo) *map E03*
213.625.8595
www.fugetsu-do.com

sun - thu 8a - 6p fri - sat 8a - 7p
treats
$ cash only. first come, first served

Yes. Please: *mochi: strawberry anco, yakiman, inaka,*
sudare, ogura, rainbow dango, mikan

I seem to have mochi on the mind these days. A while back I shot the venerable mochi store in San Francisco, **Benkyodo**, for the S.F. edition. I must admit I'm a little worried, though, about Benkyodo's experience level. After all, they've only been around since 1906. **Fugetsu-do** has been in business since 1903, which makes this small store the grandaddy of American mochi makers. Though many Americans know mochi because it's sprinkled on their fro-yo, don't let that be the only way you experience this Japanese confection. There are many varieties and flavors, each one tastier than the next.

grand central market

open-air marketplace

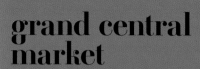

317 South Broadway
Between Third and Fourth
(Downtown) *map E04*
213.624.2378
www.grandcentralsquare.com

twitter @grandcenmrkt
mon - sun 9a - 6p
breakfast. lunch. dinner. grocery
$ first come, first served

Yes, Please: *mexican melting chocolate, chili powders, cumin, cinnamon, cactus & limes, queso fresco, dried beans, do a taco crawl!*

I'm a pretty good cook (if I do say so myself), so when a friend asked me to help her throw an engagement party, I wasn't fazed. Until she mentioned the guest list had 150 people on it. Worse, the budget was set at $300. WTF? And then I discovered **Grand Central Market**. Running through the 38 different vendor's stalls like a crazy person, I found handmade tortillas, an abundance of produce for fillings, salty Mexican cheese, and a dozen homemade moles. Dinner impossible became "feel free to bring a friend." And my under-budget delivery allowed me to stock up on spices, plus buy a juicy carnitas torta for lunch. Thanks **Grand Central Market** for helping me out.

mendocino farms

drool-worthy sandwiches

300 South Grand Avenue, Corner of Third
444 Flower Street, Corner of Fifth
(Downtown) *map E05*
213.620.1114 / 213.627.3262
www.mendocinofarms.com

twitter @mendocinofarms
see website for hours
lunch. dinner
$ first come, first served

Yes, Please: *galvanina blood orange soda; sandwiches: highway 128, curry chicken salad, rustic california, kurobuta pork belly banh mi*

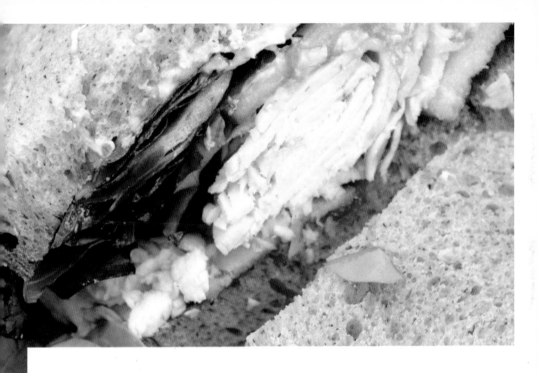

People like to gripe about driving in L.A. Seems a bit to me like living in Minnesota and complaining about the snow, but I guess people need something to complain about. In talking about **Mendocino Farms**, I often heard from people, "It's supposed to be amazing, but I'm not driving downtown for a sandwich." Still, I decided to take the journey. I got stuck in traffic and then couldn't find a parking spot. I began to silently gripe. But when I wrapped my mouth around the Rustic California sandwich—I can tell you that gridlock never tasted so good. Be brave; make the drive.

mo-chica

contemporary peruvian

3655 South Grand Avenue
Between 36th and 37th
(Downtown) *map E06*
213.747.2141
www.mo-chica.com

twitter @mo_chica
see website for hours
lunch. dinner
$$ reservations recommended

Yes, Please: *purple corn ice tea , barley ice tea with ginger & herbs, ceviche del dia, causa, papa a la huancaina, quinotto, aji de gallina, seco de cordero*

Though over the years I have perfected the art of cool nonchalance, I still enjoy a good gush. And when some-body, something or someplace makes me want to gush, then I just let it all hang out. I love **Mo-Chica**. Located in a funky food court, this place is truly off-the-beaten-path, unless you go to USC or live/work downtown. But don't let this get in your way, as this is a place to make tracks to. Chef Ricardo Zarate, who is Lima-born and London-trained, makes the most exquisite modern Peruvian food. I was so high with pleasure after eating here, my husband thought I was on drugs. I was—the **Mo-Chica** drug.

nickel diner

a new kind of diner

524 South Main Street
Between Fifth and Sixth
(Downtown) *map E07*
213.623.8301
www.nickeldiner.com

twitter @5cdiner
breakfast + lunch tue - sun 8a - 3:30p
dinner tue - sat 6 - 11p
$-$$ first come, first served

Yes, Please: *old-fashioned sodas, egg mcnickel, dutch baby pancake, donuts!!!, smac & cheese, niteclub sandwich, mama's spaghetti & meatballs*

Sometimes there's an item that I've eaten that stands out against all the other things I've stuck in my gullet while working on a book. In L.A., the winner was the crunchy-coated strawberry doughnut at **Nickel Diner**. It's so darn tasty, so totally dessert-for-breakfast, that it feels like a food item a kid would create in his imagination—something that an adult would scoff at. So for all the kids out there stuck in grown-up bodies, get yourself to **Nickel Diner** for one of these crazy good doughnuts. I'd recommend eating dessert first in this case.

ooga booga

art, printed matter, jewelry, posters, and more

**943 North Broadway #203
Between Lei Min Way and Gin Ling Way
(Chinatown)** *map S01*
**213.617.1105
www.oogaboogastore.com**

tue - sat noon - 7p

Yes, Please: *mason cooley, sarah shapiro, mika miko, mended veil, andrew jeffrey, violet hopkins, slow and steady wins the race, lucy mckenzie*

As the modern world expands with millions of cool new products, tools and technologies to make day-to-day living faster and easier, it's obvious that we are gaining efficiency. Sadly, this also means we are moving away from creating with our hands. But never fear, as **Ooga Booga** is here. This is a place that celebrates the intimate, the thoughtful and the creative. This is a place where the art of creating physical things hasn't been overshadowed by the world of mass manufacturing or electronics. Now, if you'll excuse me, I'm going to send a quick tweet about this spot.

the lazy ox canteen

casual dining with fine dining care

241 South San Pedro Street
Between Second and Third
(Little Tokyo) *map E08*
213.626.5299
www.lazyoxcanteen.com

see website for hours
lunch. brunch. dinner
$$ reservations recommended

Yes, Please: *beer flight (bartender's choice), lazy ox burger with cantal cheese and green peppercorn mustard, crispy rabbit livers, bread pudding*

While growing up, dining out meant greasy yet delicious Chinese food or hamburgers at the drugstore counter. The reason? My dad hated to dress up. Well, times they are-a-changin'. A nice restaurant no longer means wearing a tie, and lush ingredients no longer mean steep price tags. Chef/owner Josef Centeno had all of this in mind when he created the **The Lazy Ox Canteen**. He used his fine dining background and techniques to finesse dishes that are comforting yet exciting, and there are surprises—some heat, some tang. So when my dad visits, I'll be bringing him here.

wurstküche

purveyor of exotic sausages

800 East Third Street
Corner of Traction (Downtown) *map E09*
213.687.4444
www.wurstkucherestaurant.com

twitter @wurstkuche
daily 11a - midnight bar open til 2a
lunch. dinner
$-$$. first come, first served

Yes. Please: *floris apple ale, schneider edel-weisse, belgian fries; sausages: rattlesnake & rabbit with jalapeño peppers, alligator & pork, apricot & ginger, green chilies & cilantro*

Alligator & Pork, Smoked Andouille
hickory smoked, thick casing

If I could conjure up any restaurant in the world to give as a gift to my husband Wurstküche, would be it. The appeal: good beer and exotic housemade sausages. But when we approached its doors, I suddenly worried— had I been hyping it so much that the dreaded reverse effect would happen? I angsted while we ordered and perspired while waiting for the food; even the five mustard choices did nothing to quell my anxiety. But when the rattlesnake and rabbit sausage arrived, I looked at Shawn's happy face and knew everything was a-ok. Now why was I was worried?

koreatown

westlake

eat

e10 soot bull jeep

shop

s02 aardvark letterpress
s03 mother plucker feather company

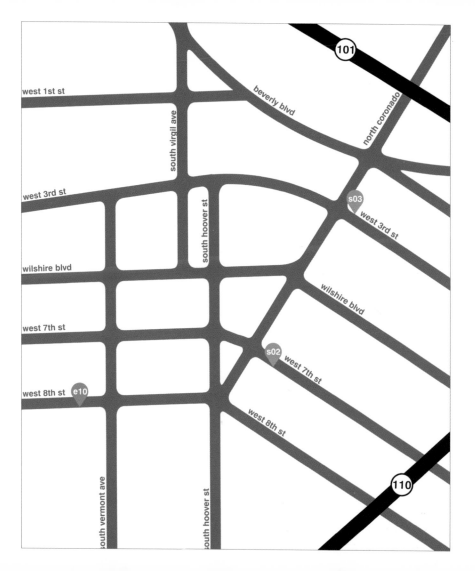

aardvark letterpress

classic, custom letterpress shop

2500 West Seventh Street
Corner of Carondelet (Westlake) *map S02*
213.388.2271
www.aardvarkletterpress.com

twitter @aardvarklp
mon - fri 10a - 5:30p sat 10a - 2p
custom orders only

figura 40

Yes, Please: *anything that is printed here:*
invitations, note cards, personal stationery, business cards

The day I visited Aardvark Letterpress was perhaps my favorite day of work I've ever had. I showed up unannounced with my sister, Amy. The incredibly gracious printer Brooks, without hesitation, proceeded to give us an extensive guided tour. Amy and I have longed for years to start our own letterpress business, so we were peeling our jaws from the ground, drooling over the Heidelberg press in action. Though sadly there's not a retail side to this operation, I will absolutely have **Aardvark** do some cards or invites for me. As for my sister, she's going to try to wrangle an apprenticeship here.

mother plucker feather company

the name says it all

2511 West Third Street
Between Coronado and Carondelet
(Westlake) *map S03*
213.637.0411
www.motherplucker.com

mon - fri 10a - 6p.

Yes, Please: *feathers: guinea hen, large eye, ring neck pheasant, almond, pheasant tail/red tip, lady amherst tail, male ostrich plume, boas*

These days when people open a business, they tend to name it something minimalistic and understated. In Willy's case, he could have easily named his spot something like Plume and called it a day. But he had a bit of fun and called it **Mother Plucker**. Ha! Love it, as this place is the mother lode of plucked plumes. Willy knows his s*#!, and whether you're in the market for pheasant, ostrich, or some other exotic variety of feather, he's got it. And even if you have no use for this type of decoration, it's well worth a trip here to see all this plumage on display.

soot bull jeep

korean charcoal bbq

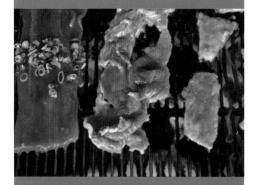

3136 West Eighth Street
Between Catalina and Kenmore
(Koreatown) *map E10*
213.387.3865

mon - sun 11a - 11p
$$ first come, first served

Yes, Please: *korean ob beer; to grill: kalbi short ribs, rib eye, squid, eel, spicy pork*

When you eat at Soot Bull Jeep, you get an extra added bonus: Eau de Soot Bull Jeep. Here's the backstory. This place is unique in the world of Korean bbq joints because their grills use coal. This creates a smoky aroma that saturates everything—from the array of eel, pork and beef cooking on your table grill to your socks. If this concerns you a bit, I can guarantee that once you start eating this food, you won't care about your post-meal scent. In fact, when people smell the Eau de **SBJ** on you, they may well ask why you smell so delicious.

highland park

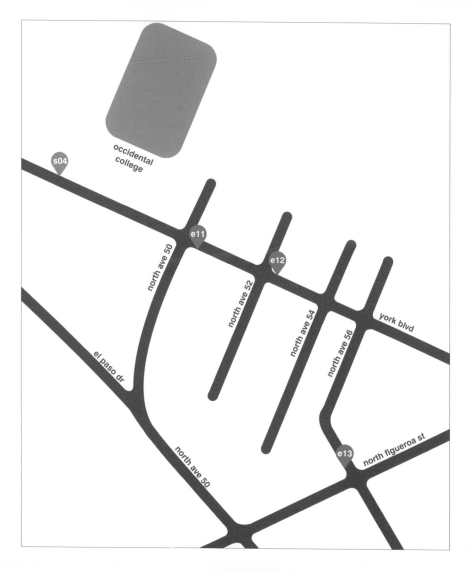

café de leche

a south american-inspired café

**5000 York Boulevard
Corner of North Avenue 50
(Highland Park)** *map E11*
**323.551.6828
www.cafedeleche.net**

twitter @cafe_de_leche
sun - thu 7a - 6p fri - sat 7a - 7p
coffee / tea. snacks
$ first come, first served

Yes, Please: *horchata with espresso, organic agave mocha, organic mate latte, organic hot chocolate, banana nut muffin, dulce de leche kiss*

Part of the fun of L.A. can certainly be "the scene," which is nearly impossible to avoid if you're going out and about eating and drinking. But unless you are a complete scene-a-phant, there are times when you need to get away from the scariness and find a quiet place where people go to actually drink coffee. **Café de Leche** is one of these no-nonsense, settle in with your newspaper and enjoy a good cup of coffee spots. I dare you to spot a posturer who's scanning the room behind dark shades. Go ahead and breathe in the fresh, attitude-free air around you. Ahhhhhhh...

el huarache azteca

home of the huarache

5225 York Boulevard
Between North Ave 52 and North Ave 53
(Highland Park) *map E12*
323.478.9572

daily 8am - 10pm
breakfast. lunch. dinner
$ cash only. first come, first served

Yes, Please: *jamaica agua fresca, horchata, consomme de borrego, chilaquiles, veggie torta, huaraches: pork adobada, carne asada*

I remember the first time I ate at a dive. It was in high school, and I was with an adventurous friend. I eyed the peeling paint, what looked like a shady clientele and the perceived scary menu. I was petrified. Since that time I've learned that peeling paint is really "patina," that shady clientele are often food-loving insiders who want to keep their gem a secret and that scary menus often feature amazing food. So I love **El Huarache Azteca**. I devoured the huaraches (Mexican pizzas), dousing everything with salsas from the (seemingly shady) salsa bar. I love this dive, peeling paint and all.

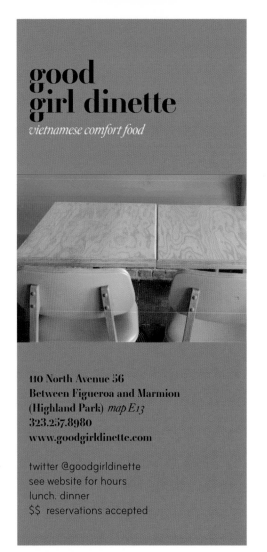

good
girl dinette

vietnamese comfort food

110 North Avenue 56
Between Figueroa and Marmion
(Highland Park) *map E13*
323.257.8980
www.goodgirldinette.com

twitter @goodgirldinette
see website for hours
lunch. dinner
$$ reservations accepted

Yes, Please: *housemade sodas, vietnamese-style coffee, rice cakes with crispy scallion tofu, slow-roasted pork baguette, grandpa's porridge*

The last time I ate a chicken pot pie I was probably in junior high, and it was the tin-lined frozen variety with chunky peas and carrots and dry chicken. Not exactly gourmet, but comforting and strangely delicious all the same. When I spotted the chicken pot pie on the menu at **Good Girl Dinette**, I decided it was time for a revisit. I think it was the best thing I had eaten in weeks, maybe months. I sat there and blew on the still-hot bites, unable to stop devouring the curry-rich chicken and perfect crust. Pot pie paradise can be yours at **Good Girl Dinette**.

society of the spectacle

groovy eyewear

**4563 York Boulevard
Between Avenue 46 and Eagle Rock
(Highland Park)** *map S04*
**323.255.4300
www.societyspectacle.com**

mon - fri 11a - 7p sat 10a - 6p
sun noon - 5p

Yes, Please: *sunglasses & glasses: ray ban, salt optics, oliver peoples, l.a. eyewear, kaenon, paul smith, dita, mosley tribes, kirk originals, persol, vintage*

You don't need to be a genius to figure out this is a town of sunglasses. Yes, there is plenty of sun here to warrant the use of protective eyewear—but this is also a place where folks wear sunglasses at midnight to (try and) look cool. Whatever the reason you wear them, the place to buy sunglasses and just plain old glasses is **Society of the Spectacle**. The sisters behind S of the S have 30 years experience in the sunglasses industry, so they know their stuff. Plus, I love that many of the lines they stock are California-based, so you're getting a truly authentic Golden State experience here.

atwater village

broome street general store

coffee bar and beautiful pantry items

2912 Rowena Avenue
Between Avenel and Herkimer
(Silver Lake) *map E14*
323.570.0405

twitter @broomestgeneral
mon - sat 8a - 8p sun 8a - 6p
coffee/tea. grocery
$-$$ first come, first served

Yes, Please: *san marzano tomato sauce, la tourangelle oils, mcclure's pickles, madagascar bourbon vanilla extract, stanley thermoses, broome street spices*

Sophie Esteban created her dream pantry in an apartment on Broome Street during her time as a New Yorker.
She would spend hours sourcing favorite spices from Chinatown and all the best goodies from Little Italy—she scoured NYC high and low and found all of its food treasures. When she relocated to the West Coast it seemed a shame to let all that great research go to waste, so she opened **Broome Street General Store**. This place is packed with everything one might need in a kitchen, from Weck canning jars and Meyer's cleaning products to Morris Kitchen ginger syrup (for Moscow Mules!) and Sophie's favorite fleur de sel from Saunier de Camargue. It's a little bit of kitchen heaven.

canelé

farmers' market fresh food

3219 Glendale Boulevard
Between Brunswick and Edenhurst
(Atwater Village) *map E15*
323.666.7133
www.canele-la.com

twitter @canele_la
see website for hours
brunch. dinner
$$-$$$ first come, first served

Yes. Please: *concord grape mimosa, lamill coffee, pecan sticky bun, baked pancake, persimmon salad, eggs en cocotte, open-faced blt*

Sometimes when you go out to eat, do you secretly hope the food is going to taste like a delicious home-cooked meal? So why not then just stay at home and cook? Because few of us can cook a meal the way we idealize it to taste, so we search for the someone who can. Chef Corina at **Canelé** is that someone. Take her roast chicken or her three-egg omelette—simple, perfectly executed and deliciously fulfilling food that is the essence of a "home-cooked meal." The only problem here is this: which to order first, the chicken or the egg?

french general
vintage fabrics, notions and papers

2009 Riverside Drive
Off of the Glendale and Golden State
Freeways (Silverlake) *map S05*
323.668.0488
www.frenchgeneral.com

mon 11a - 4p
online shopping. workshops. special events

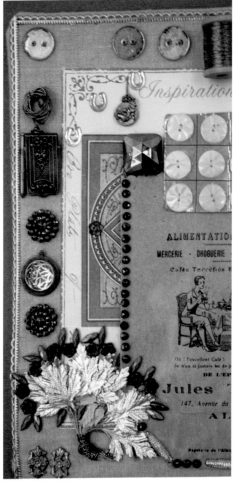

Yes, Please: *sewing charm bracelet kit, rouenneries fabric collection, lavender travel pillows, grain sack bags, vintage linen sheets*

My sisters and I recently started a craft blog (wanton self-promotion here: bbbcraft.blogspot.com). It's mostly about sharing the various doodads and whatnots we like to make. I'll admit our collective dream is to someday be full-time crafters. In other words, we are totally jealous of Kaari. Her store **French General** is soooo pretty, filled with fabrics and notions and vintage papers that would make any crafter swoon deeply. Her books and kits are hugely inspirational for us crafties. And if crafting isn't your thing, no worries—there's plenty here for you as well. **French General**, I've got a crush on you.

palate food + wine

restaurant and wine bar with amazing eats

**933 South Brand Boulevard
Between Acacia and Garfield
(Glendale)** *map E16*
**818.662.9463
www.palatefoodwine.com**

see website for hours
$$-$$$ reservations accepted

Yes, Please: *08 domaine la bastide viognier, 07 organic fouquet vouvray sec le marigny, pickled turnip & beets, porkfolio, potted lamb*

I've always been better at baking than cooking, thanks to my aptitude for precision, and no thanks to my lack of talent for winging it. If, however, I could cook with great skill, I would want to make the kind of food Chef Octavio makes at **Palate Food + Wine**. I found myself taking notes not just for this book but for my own personal uses—wondering if I could recreate the sweet potato gnocchi with sage, celery and chestnuts, with a light grating of spicy pecans on top to give it a kick. In the long run I think I'll stick to my quick breads and pizza dough and let the experts at **Palate** do the cooking.

viet noodle bar

northern-style vietnamese

3133 Glendale Boulevard
Between Glenfeliz and Edenhurst
(Atwater Village) *map E17*
323.906.1575

twitter @vietnoodlebar
daily 11a - 10p
$-$$ cash only. first come, first served

Yes, Please: *pennywort green juice, housemade organic soymilk, vietnamese coffee, white fish noodle, lemongrass organic chicken sandwich*

I have three words for you: housemade soy milk. This menu item at **Viet Noodle Bar** might pass you by if you let it, but you would be making a whopping culinary mistake. While I could happily dine on the sandwiches and pho every day, my favorite thing here is the organic soy milk. The owner and chef, Viet, makes it by handcrushing soy beans, fermenting them, and then infusing them with herbs and spices. He is a craftsman of northern Vietnamese cuisine, where the food is simple, gently spiced and extremely seasonal. I'm just happy to know that his soy milk is in season any time of the year.

silver lake

los feliz, echo park

eat

shop

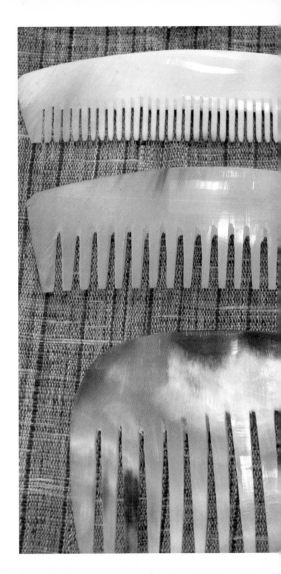

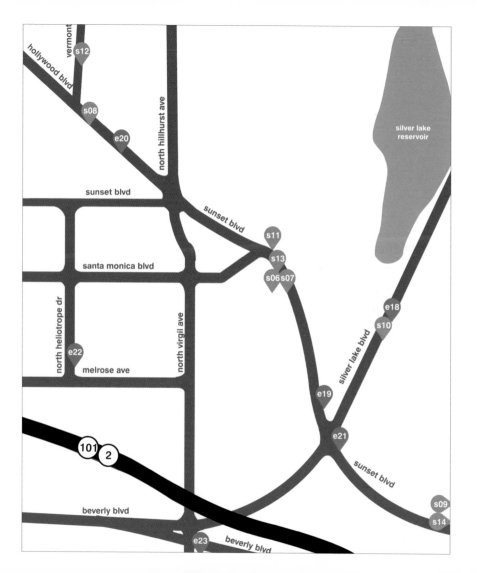

bar keeper

everything for the modern bar

**3910 West Sunset Boulevard
Corner of Hyperion Avenue
(Silver Lake)** *map S06*
**323.669.1675
www.barkeepersilverlake.com**

mon - thu noon - 6p
fri - sat 11a – 7p sun 11a – 6p

Yes, Please: *scrappy's lavender bitters, mid-century vintage shakers, death's door whisky, mister mojito muddler, bulleit bourbon, dirty sue martini mix*

Although I don't think Don Draper is a model husband, I do believe we have gotten a little lazy on the cocktail front. It's time to ditch the wine and take a few tips from the boys over at the fictional Sterling Cooper. You can do this by visiting **Bar Keeper**, where you'll be inspired to become an at-home mixologist. My sad little bar cart needs to be filled with almost every item in this store, from the array of mid-century shakers to the local spirits and housemade bitters. I'm ditching the rosé this summer and will instead drink whiskey sours and moscow mules using **Bar Keeper's** assortment of small batch liquors and stylish accoutrements.

casbah café and bazaar

moroccan bazaar

3900 West Sunset Boulevard
Corner of Hyperion (Silver Lake) *map S07*
323.664.7000
www.casbahcafe.com

daily 6a - 11p

Yes, Please: *camel leather shoes, stitched silk cloths, embroidered tunics, woven & beaded necklaces, hair combs, printed tablecloths, an afternoon treat at the charming café*

On the other side of the globe, things are different: different temperatures, different modes of transportation, different neighborhood cafés. But step into **Casbah Café** and you'll feel like you've covered the distance in no time flat. Suddenly you're in a café in the middle of Morocco, Algeria, Egypt, or Turkey. Even better, this café contains a bazaar, offering up silk wraps, leather sandals, tortoise shell combs, and a variety of imported treasures, many of them custom made just for this store. All this and you've only traveled the distance from your car to **Casbah**.

jake
vintage styles for men

4644 Hollywood Boulevard
Between Vermont and Hillhurst
(Los Feliz) *map S08*
323.662.5253
www.jakevintage.com

tue - sat noon - 7p sun noon - 5p

Yes, Please: *vintage: suits, ties, sport coats, trousers, plaid shirts, hats, cuff links, accessories*

I often see stores when I'm researching a city that seem as though someone had the off-the-cuff thought, "How cool would it be to own a store?" and then set up shop in a half-baked way, with slat walls, plastic hangers and no specific point of view. Imagine this, then picture the opposite, and you have **Jake**. There couldn't be a more carefully conceived, edited, merchandised, and displayed store than this. Owner Jonathan Kanarek long dreamed of creating this store with its lounge-cum-dressing-room vibe. Men, if vintage wear from the '40s to '60s is your bag, then **Jake** is your place.

kellygreen home

goods for a green life

2149 Sunset Boulevard
At Alvarado (Echo Park) *map S09*
2525 Main Street, Space 102
At Ocean Park (Santa Monica)
ep 213.353.0488 / sm 310.450.6464
www.kellygreenhome.com

twitter @kellygreenhome
tue – sun 11a – 7p
green design services

Yes, Please: *alchemy, every book about green living you'll ever need, compact solar chargers, spools of twine, laura zindel ceramics, urban indoor composters*

Having only one job is soooo last decade. Take it from Kelly, who runs her own interior design company and these incredible, all-things-green shops. More and more people I know are diversifying—out of necessity, boredom or just plain interest—and creating multiple careers for themselves. If a second or third career isn't in the works for you this year, why not take your new year's resolutions one step at a time and go green? The first stop: **Kellygreen**, of course, where there are enough products, books and ideas to get you started on the right path.

lake

lovely women's boutique

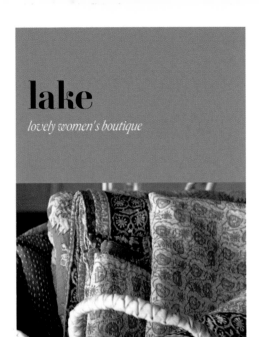

1618-1/2 Silver Lake Boulevard
Near Effie
(Silver Lake) *map S10*
323.664.6522
www.lakeboutique.com/.com

twitter @lakeboutique
tue - sat noon - 7p sun noon - 5p
online shopping

Yes, Please: *by malene birger, ever, mm6, matta, le mont st. michel, vpl, etoile, raquel allegra, isabel marant, sendra, barr co., tatine, improvd*

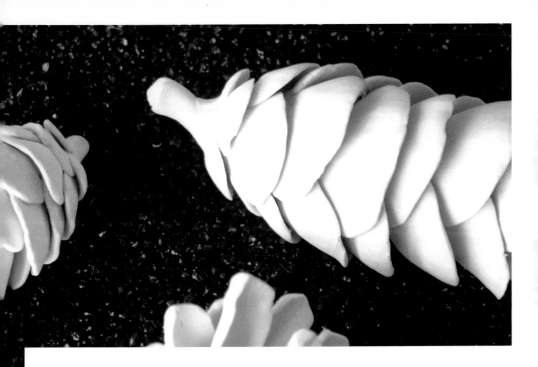

There are some stores you want to shop in and others you want to transfer all the goods right into your home. Lake is the latter as it makes sense to me to just take everything here, since I like it all. What's so great about this clothing/apothecary/lifestyle store? Basically all of the components of a well-stocked closet are here. If Melissa won't let me take the whole kit and caboodle in one fell swoop, maybe I'll just slip into some of the clothing and position myself somewhere in the store as a living mannequin and make myself useful.

lamill coffee

serious coffee

1636 Silver Lake Boulevard
Corner of Effie (Silver Lake) *map E18*
323.663.4441
www.lamillcoffee.com

twitter @lamillcoffee
sun - thu 7a - 10p fri - sat 7a - 11p
breakfast. lunch. dinner. coffee / tea.
$ first come, first served

Yes, Please: *coffee extractions: chemex, siphon brew, french press; hong kong milk tea, house-made brioche doughnut holes, huevos "blanchet," sofia panini*

In my current preggy state, I can take in stride the ever-expanding belly and the elimination of certain foods—cutting alcohol hasn't even gotten me down. But I deeply mourn the demise of my daily coffee habit. When I stopped into **Lamill Coffee** for breakfast one morning, I threw all discipline out the window and got the very largest coffee on the menu. I twitched with excitement as I watched it brew in front of me. When it came time to drink it, I relished every drop like it was liquid gold. And though my doctor might not have approved, my baby now knows what really good coffee is.

lark cake shop

super sweet cake and cupcake shop

3337 West Sunset Boulevard
Corner of Micheltorena
(Silver Lake) *map E19*
323.667.2968
www.larkcakeshop.com

sun - mon noon - 6p tue - thu 10a - 8p
fri - sat 10a - 10p
treats
$-$$ first come, first served

Yes, Please: *cupcakes: sara's famous chocolate mousse, old-fashioned ice box, colleen's caramel, red velvet, berry shortcake; cakes: carrot cake, black & white cake*

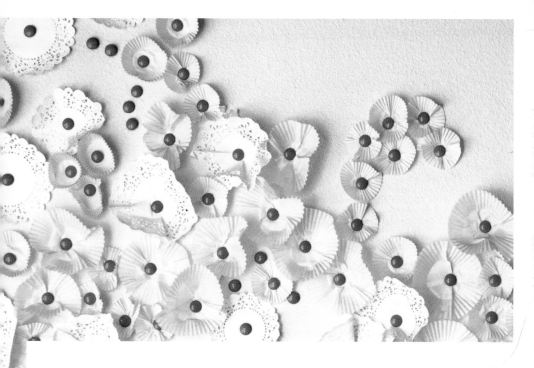

When I started working on this book, I would have sworn to you that I wouldn't put in a cupcake spot. It's not that I don't love a good cupcake, but cupcake places have multiplied like rabbits, and many are average at best. Then I discovered **Lark Cake Shop**, which is truly special (technically, it's a cake and cupcake spot, so I felt like I wasn't breaking my early rule, btw). The edible gems here are just the right size and perfectly moist, with an appropriate frosting-to-cake ratio. And they've got nifty wrappers that make eating them oh-so-easy to devour without a mess. I'm re-embracing the cupcake.

mohawk general store/amsterdam modern

eclectic mix of fashion and mid-century housewares and furniture

**4011 West Sunset Boulevard
Between Santa Monica and Sanborn
(Silver Lake)** *map S 11*
**323.669.1601
www.mohawkgeneralstore.net
www.amsterdammodern.com**

twitter @mohawkgeneral
mon - sat 11a - 7p sun noon - 6p
online shopping

Yes, Please: *gitman vintage shirts, rachel comey shoes, jasmine shokrian, cire trudon candles, moscot sunglasses, vintage school maps, '40s audio equipment*

I first met Kevin Carney ten years ago in a downtown New York space where he showed me his line of cozy graphic sweatshirts. I bumped into him years later here in LA and we discussed his favorite dj gigs. Last I heard, he had a new shoe line. When I stumbled upon **Mohawk General Store**, it was no surprise that it was his store, as it combined all his talents and hobbies. Kevin and his wife Bo teamed up with Ellen LeComte at **Amsterdam Modern** to create a two-stores-in-one/something-for-everyone experience with their eclectic mix of modern furniture, vintage audio equipment, clothing, and accessories. I dare you not to be drawn in here just like I was.

new high (m)art

where fashion favorites meet outdoor chic

**1720 North Vermont Avenue
Corner of Kingswell
(Los Feliz)** *map S12*
**323.638.0271
www.newhighmart.com**

twitter @newhighmart
mon - fri noon - 8p
sat noon - 7p sun 2 - 7p
online shopping

Yes, Please: *lauren manoogian sweaters & jewelry, mm6 dresses, wool & the gang yarn, so. american folk towels, felt mountain hats, bernhard wilhelm for camper footwear*

Each item in New High (M)art has a story behind it, and Richard and Miho are the storytellers. Influenced by the world of fashion with an outdoorsy, nomadic sensibility, this store is filled with finds from this twosome's worldwide travels. Whether hiking in Peru, driving along Lake Michigan or strolling along St. Honore, they are uncovering emerging designers and talented artisans and bringing their beautiful wares to showcase in NH(M). This intriguing retail environment is sure to inspire—perhaps to dress in a romantically bohemian style and drink prosecco along the Arno or throw on your hiking boots (same outfit of course) and head to Machu Picchu—take your pick of a well-dressed adventure.

mother dough

authentic neapolitan pizza

4648 Hollywood Boulevard
Between Rodney and Vermont
(Los Feliz) *map E20*
323.644.2885
www.motherdoughpizza.com

tue - sun 6 - 11p
dinner
$$ first come, first served

Yes, Please: *duck crostini, burrata salad, oven-roasted vine tomato pizza, prosciutto and arugula pizza, oven-roasted pears, triple chocolate mousse, brother thelonious ale*

Being married to an Italian, I feel like it is my responsibility to immediately visit all the new pizza restaurants in this town. Hence why I was excited when **Mother Dough** opened. Iranian born Bez Campani got a taste for Neapolitan style pizza while living in Milan, and after moving here, he launched a search to find the perfect slice. Alas, he never found it and so he decided to make it himself. He alone mans the oven and carefully nurtures the dough using a starter he's had for ten years. He then marries his beautiful dough with buffalo mozzarella flown in from Naples and throws on other carefully sourced toppings, baking the pie at a blistering high heat in a custom built oven for exactly 60 seconds. What a masterpiece.

pho café

*a place for pho and vietnamese
home cooking*

**2841 West Sunset Boulevard
At Silver Lake Boulevard
(Silver Lake)** *map E 21*
213.413.0888

daily 11a - midnight
lunch. dinner
$-$$ cash only. first come, first served

Yes, Please: *vietnamese coffee, 33 beer, fresh homemade
limeade, goi cuon, banh xeo, pho tai, pho tai bo vien,
bun cha gio tom thit nuong, dac biet*

My friend Annie, who is now one of the co-editors of this book, likes to give specific, ornately detailed food descriptions. Not only will she regale you with the 10 things she loves on any given menu, she can also list the 12 things she has tried and is not so excited about. To add to her L.A. eating cred, there's almost nowhere in this town she hasn't eaten. So, when she casually mentioned to me that the Vietnamese crepe at **Pho Café** was maybe her favorite menu item anywhere in town, I was on my way before she could finish her sentence. Though Annie can exaggerate a bit, this crepe wasn't unfairly hyped. It was crazy good.

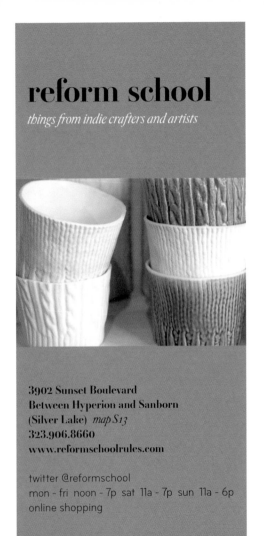

reform school

things from indie crafters and artists

3902 Sunset Boulevard
Between Hyperion and Sanborn
(Silver Lake) *map S13*
323.906.8660
www.reformschoolrules.com

twitter @reformschool
mon - fri noon - 7p sat 11a - 7p sun 11a - 6p
online shopping

Yes, Please: *kg + ab porcelain mixed nuts, alyssa ettinger ceramic knit coaster set, k studio pillows, hillery sproatt mobile, magno wooden radio*

Ever since I was in grad school for journalism, I've dreamed of being the editor-in-chief at a craft magazine. The first thing I would do at the helm of this fantasy mag would be to source all of my talent and ideas from the brilliant creatives whose goods can be found at **Reform School**. This is a place where everything on display has been rethought and reformed for the new millennium. Where smart, thoughtful and wicked creative crafting is a long way away from grandma's knit tea cozies and macramé doilies. Though I'm long done with school, I'm just getting started at **Reform School**.

scoops

housemade ice cream with flavors that change daily

712 North Heliotrope Drive
At Melrose (Wilshire Center) *map E22*
323.906.2649

mon - sat noon - 10p sun 2 - 6p
treats
$ cash only. first come, first served

Yes, Please: *brown bread & virgil's root beer float;*
ice cream & sorbets: blackberry jasmine, coconut lemon-
grass, guinness & tiramisu

A cop, a hipster, two businessmen, a bike messenger, and me. What food and place could attract such a wide variety of people and palates? Ice cream at **Scoops**. Why here: There's a varietal cornucopia of ice cream made fresh here daily, from simple yet unusual flavors such as salt and honey to the outré green tea and ricotta cheese. With all this to choose from, I had a root beer float. Sounds boring to you? Try it with Virgil's root beer and brown bread ice cream. At **Scoops**, there is something for everyone. Just don't get your heart set on anything because it will be gone tomorrow.

tavin

vintage boutique

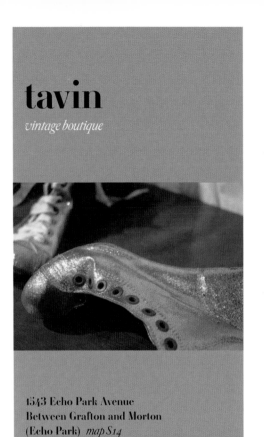

1543 Echo Park Avenue
Between Grafton and Morton
(Echo Park) *map S14*
213.482.5832
www.lifebytavin.com

twitter @lifebytavin
tue - sun noon - 7p

Yes, Please: *tavin redesigned vintage, tavin bridal, danceteria necklace; vintage: yohji yamomoto, valentino, boho batik, christian dior, comme des garçons*

What does it mean when you say somebody or something is a "true original"? Instead of putting it into words, just go to **Tavin** and meet the owner Erin. Shopping here is like being in the midst of an interactive art installation where the theme is Erin's vision of vintage. I think this place is perhaps the most expressive and intricately staged vintage shop I've come across; every piece is allowed to tell its own glorious story. Be sure though, when you visit, to give yourself enough time to browse, and then browse again. Soaking up the big picture is a wondrous journey.

valerie
confections

chocolate and toffee

**3360 West First Street
Between Virgil and Beverly
(Silverlake)** *map E23*
**213.739.8149
www.valerieconfections.com**

twitter @valerieconfctns
mon - sat 10a - 6p
treats
$ first come, first served

VALERIE
at the market

*Fancy
Kumqua B*

NET WEIGHT 8 oz (226 grams)

Yes, Please: *toffee noir, milk toffee, almond toffee treats, salt & pepper truffles, almond fleur de sel toffee, mint mendiants; apricot, yellow peach & kumquat jam*

I don't know the PR geniuses who started putting word out that chocolate is good for you, but I love them. I believe them. I trust their every word. In my world, chocolate is the new penicillin. So when I learned that **Valerie**, the lovely chocolatier whose confections I'd been admiring in various shops across the country, had her own little shop, I raced to it, knowing it was just what the doctor ordered. These pure, high-quality chocolates, toffees and truffles are exquisitely beautiful and deliciously unmatched. No marketing spin was needed to convince me of this: **Valerie Confections** are good for you.

hollywood

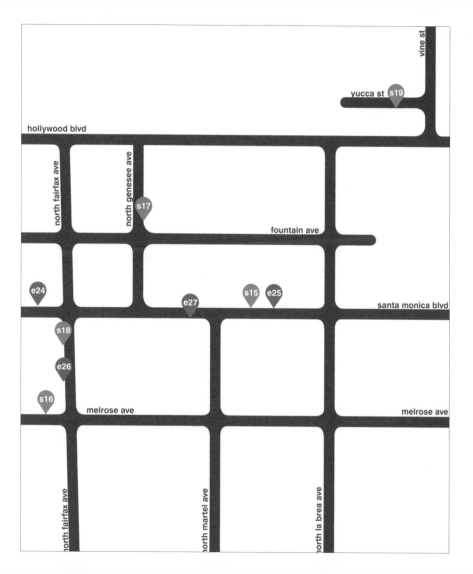

baby blues b.b.q.

best ribs and fixins' in town

7953 Santa Monica Boulevard
Corner of Hayworth
(West Hollywood) *map E24*
323.656.1277
www.babyblueswh.com

twitter @babybluesbbq
see website for hours and venice location
lunch. dinner
$$ reservations accepted for parties of six

Yes, Please: *the tackle box: 2 grilled shrimp, 2 hush puppies, 2 fried green tomatoes, & 4 wings; fixins: mac & cheese, collard greens & cornbread; baby back ribs platter*

If owner Danny Fischer's energy could be bottled up and sold, he'd make billions. And if he bottled up and sold his b.b.q. sauces, well.... he'd also be rich. **Baby Blues B.B.Q.** is what happens when a guy whose dad owned a barbeque joint (Danny) meets a guy whose dad owned a soul food restaurant (Rick) and they make a baby. AKA, heaven. And their passion isn't just for the food, which is legit, it's also for service. I have never felt more taken care of than I do here. So I keep going back... for baby backs!

church

statement-making clothing, jewelry and accessories

7277 Santa Monica Boulevard
Corner of Greenacre
(West Hollywood) *map S15*
323.876.8887
www.churchboutique.com

mon - fri 11a - 7p sat 11a - 6p

Yes, Please: *jennifer mary, raquel allegra, coquette, liana reid, endovanera, little doe, cerre, riser goodwyn*

Growing up, I went with my dad to just about every variety of church you could imagine: Greek Orthodox, Southern Baptist, Maranatha—even coffeehouse varieties that didn't meet in an actual church. It was quite the education. But I've never been to a church like this **Church**. I saw immediately why people worship here. It's like owners David and Rodney have created a new kind of religion, showing fresh perspectives from the fashion world. I felt my horizons opening to exciting new worlds. This **Church** is one I could really get excited about.

creatures of comfort

both indie and established women's clothing

7971 Melrose Avenue
Between Edinburgh and Hayworth
(West Hollywood) *map S16*
323.655.7855
www.creaturesofcomfort.us

twitter @creaturesnyla
mon - sat 11a - 7p sun noon - 6p
online shopping

Yes, Please: *manu jewelry, acne, étoile isabel marant, vpl underwear, maptote bags, zero + maria cornejo, apc, united bamboo*

I am a creature of comfort. When I wake up on a Saturday morning and I'm hanging around the house, I tend to pull on a pair of sweats or leggings and a soft t-shirt rather than a pair of skinny jeans and a structured shirt. Even when I venture outside the house, an occasion when style comes first, comfort is a close second. This is why I'm fond of **Creatures of Comfort**. Style is at the forefront here with some very sharp brands, but this goes hand-in-hand with everything being extremely wearable. I'm so comfortable in this store, I wish I never had to leave.

food + lab

organic, european cafe

7253 Santa Monica Boulevard
Between Fuller and Formosa
(West Hollywood) *map E25*
See website for Silver Lake location
323.851.7120
www.foodlabcatering.com

twitter @foodlab
mon - fri 8a - 8p sat - sun 8a - 7p
$-$$ first come, first served

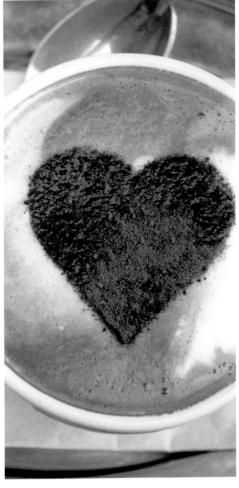

Yes. Please: *almdudler soda, imported nutella, deluscious cookies, housemade swiss bircher muesli with berries, fingerling potatoes*

Years ago I visited a beautiful mountain town on the border of Italy and Austria called Bolzano. This place was a wonderful mash-up of Italian food, wine and beautiful scenery with the organized, solid design sense of the Austrians. Two diverse cultures blending together. This is the case with **Food + Lab**, where the SoCal menu is injected with Austrian specialties, like muesli, homemade Austrian meatloaf and Vienna Kaffee. The focus is organic, fresh food, and the market shelves are stocked with specialty foodstuffs, local and imported alike. This melting pot makes up one tasty place.

house on genesee

a family-run store, gallery, café and more

1300 North Genesee
Corner of Fountain
(West Hollywood) *map S17*
323.845.9821
www.houseongenesee.com

twitter @houseongenesee
appointment only
special events

Yes, Please: *artless furniture, gabriela artigas jewelry, bang buro, farm tactics, zan zan eyewear, taller flora by carla fernandez*

You will leave House on Genesee with two emotions. The first will be complete jaw-dropping awe. The second will be jealousy that you aren't the fourth Artigas sibling. This immensely talented family has created a house that is not a home, but a store, a place to eat and a studio. Alex crafts the furniture, Gabriela the jewelry and Tere the fresh juice you will enjoy in respite in the peaceful backyard. Everything you might desire is in this magical house. Everything, that is, except the adoption papers for what would make you an adjunct Artigas family member.

iko iko

thematic hi-craft

931 North Fairfax Avenue
Between Willoughby and Romaine
(West Hollywood) *map S18*
323.719.1079
www.ikoikospace.com

tue - sat noon - 7p sun noon - 5p
online shopping

Yes, Please: *rowena sartin (the house line), hannah keefe soldered jewelry, waka waka furniture & objects, wb /rs necklaces, wa rousoku candles, vintage design books*

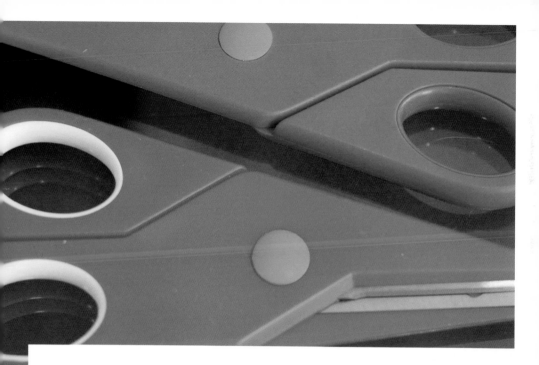

As any of the authors of these books will tell you, when writing we often find ourselves using the same words to describe items or places. Sure, we can pull out the thesaurus and dig around, but usually this yields pretty bland results. For a while now I've been looking for the perfect term to describe small-batch, artist-based designs, and then Kristin at **Iko Iko** handed the term to me on a platter: hi-craft. Yes, yes, YES! Of course she would have coined this, because her ever-evolving space (her store theme changes every six weeks or so) is a mecca of hi-craft. All hail Kristin.

lindy & grundy

local & organic butcher shop

801 North Fairfax Avenue
Between Waring and Willoughby
(West Hollywood) *map E26*
323.951.0804
www.lindyandgrundy.com

twitter @lindygrundy
tue - sat 11a - 7:30p sun 11a - 5p
butcher. grocery
$-$$ first come, first served

Yes. Please: *bacon stock, olympic provisions salamis, sonoma direct lamb, rancho san julian beef, faux hanger steaks, smoked chicken legs, cowgirl creamery cheese*

When I was little I had a pet cow named Salt & Pepper and I loved her. And then she was slaughtered and yes, I ate her. The lovely married team at **Lindy & Grundy** also have a healthy respect for animals (until recently, owner Amelia was a vegetarian) by being passionately committed to whole-animal butchery. This is both sustainable (yes shoppers, chicken necks are excellent fried!) and admirable. And with that respect comes enthusiasm that they share on a daily basis with their customers by educating without lecturing and offering amazing butchery workshops. In your memory **Salt & Pepper**, I will shop here.

lost & found stores

collection of stores for women, men and children

6314 - 6324 Yucca Street
Between Ivar and Vine
(Hollywood) *map S19*
323.856.5872
www.lostandfoundshop.com

twitter @lostandfound_la
mon - sat 10a - 6p
registries

Yes, Please: *local, repetto, aris geldis, lucky fish, missoni home, liberty rose, jerome dreyfusmaria la rosa, sydney's pottery*

It's possible that one day we'll wake up and Jamie Rosenthal will have taken over L.A. As we speak, her little empire of **Lost & Found** is ever growing on Yucca Street, with a gallery, a men's store and her quintessential women's and children's outposts. Walking into any of these places feels like being on the other side of the wardrobe door, and though you may feel as if you've landed in a magical land, you will still be firmly planted in Jamie's world. I apologize for having only three meager pictures to illustrate how fantastic this world is. This just means you'll have to get yourself here posthaste.

salt's cure

comfortable californian charcuterie
and wine bar

7494 Santa Monica Boulevard
Corner of Gardner
(West Hollywood) *map E27*
323.850.7258
www.saltscure.com

twitter @saltscure
daily 11a - 3p, 5:30 - 10:30p
lunch. brunch. dinner. grocery
$$ reservations recommended

Yes. Please: *oatmeal griddle cakes, pickle plate, pretzel roll, smoked halibut, tamworth liver & yorkshire head cheese terrine, grass-fed burger with fries, strawberry pie*

When you find out that two guys who used to work at your favorite restaurant (The Hungry Cat) opened their own place, you don't walk, you run. So I did, with high expectations, high tail it to **Salt's Cure**, and I wasn't disappointed. One thing that struck me at this cozy farm-to-table restaurant was its serious "guy" vibe, so my husband recently had a man date here. Greg and his friend sat at the bar, sharing house-made charcuterie and other meaty delights. Both commented that the open kitchen was better viewing than a football flat-screen, proving that food trumps sport.

mid-city east

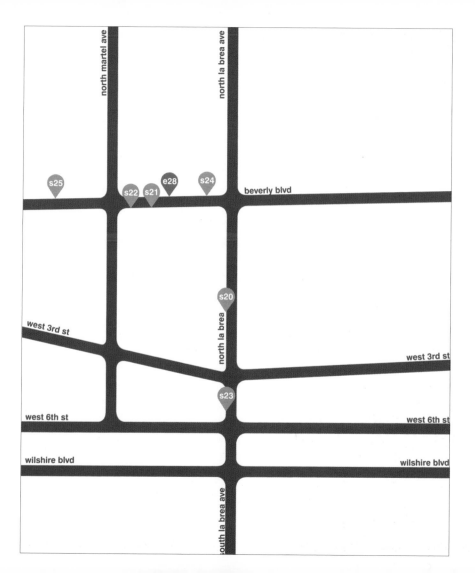

angelini
osteria

simple, sublime italian

7313 Beverly Boulevard
Between Fuller and Pointsettia
(Mid-City) *map E28*
323.297.0070
www.angeliniosteria.com

lunch tue - fri noon - 2:30p
dinner tue - sun 5:30 - 10:30p
$$-$$$ reservations accepted

Yes, Please: *felsina chianti classico riserva, fresh ancho-vies with artichokes & red beets, pumpkin tortelli, lasagna verde "omaggio nonna elvira"*

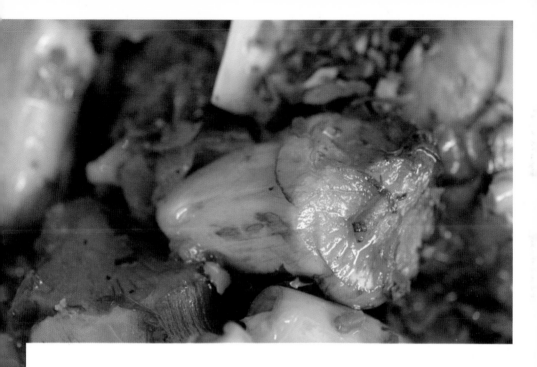

Common to Los Angeles are large-scale restaurants with sometimes over-the-top décor, high attention to image and only second or sometimes third-degree attention to the food itself. It's with supreme pleasure, then, to go to a place like **Angelini Osteria**, where the atmosphere is intimate yet no-nonsense, and one hundred percent of the attention and focus is put on the food. This seminal Italian restaurant was featured in a number of the editions *eat.shop los angeles*, and it continues to win us over years later, and will continue to for years to come.

feal mor

*french and japanese menswear, vintage
military and housewares*

165 South La Brea Avenue
Between 1st and 2nd
(Mid-City) *map S20*
323.939.6600
www.fealmor.com

twitter @fealmor
mon - sat 11a - 7p sun noon - 5p
online shopping

Yes, Please: *feal mor clothing, gato heroi surfboards, vintage restored bikes, eric darrow ceramics, everyw'air room sprays, kathryn hermann vintage batik tea towels*

The romantic tale of J.P Plunier is something out of a Merchant Ivory film. He hales from Brittany in France, home of the famous Breton striped shirt (think Coco Chanel in her weekend attire), and now lives in Claremont, CA, surrounded by talented artists and artisans. His shop is stocked with their creations—many both useful and beautiful—as well as his own menswear line inspired by the sea. The **Feal Mor** (translating to "of the sea") line consists of all things striped and nautical—cozy sweaters, basic striped t-shirts and pea coats. The pottery, jewelry, surfboards and bikes that fill his store inspire me to fill my life with both creative people and objects.

gibson

both art and interiors

7350 Beverly Boulevard
Corner of Fuller (Mid-City) *map S 21*
323.934.4248
www.garygibson.com

twitter @garygibsonid
mon - fri 9a - 6p sat 11a - 5p

Yes, Please: *gibson studio furniture; artists: jim gentry, michael koch, nancy levy, alissa warshaw, michael shemchuk, donald robson*

It's hard for me to really get seduced by a white-walled, starkly lit, sterile art gallery. Though the art on the walls might be enticing, I find the experience too disconnected from how the art might look in my home. At **Gibson**, artwork mingles with found objects, vintage furniture and a variety of unexpected items. Aha! This is what I'm talking about. Here I can get the sense of how pieces would work in my world. I liked **Gibson** so much, I wondered if I could move in. Seems that's not an option, but I can use the design services of the folks here to help me recreate my own **Gibson** feel at home.

ige
artful lifestyle store

7382 Beverly Boulevard
Between Martel and Fuller
(Mid-City) *map S22*
323.939.2788
www.igedesign.com

mon - sat 11a - 6p
online shopping

Yes, Please: *ige designs: canvas calendar, laser-cut mobiles, pillows, humpty & eggberta dumpty stuffed toys; k studio pouches & books, dbo home ceramics*

I just read a newspaper story about a recall of children's jewelry made with a toxic and carcinogenic metal. Yikes. How far removed have we become from the people and places that make our goods that this sort of thing happens?! At **Ige**, you are barely one step removed. Witness Helene, who works at the back of her store, putting together her amazing mobiles. And most other objects sold here are made by hand—by real people, not by real big factories. Everything here feels like an individual work of art. And nontoxic art at that.

The house I grew up in is a turn-of-the-century Tudor. Living in a place with leaded glass windows and vintage plumbing meant numerous trips to big old hardware stores that specialized in vintage fittings. So even though I might have thought these trips were pretty ho-hum as a child, I now love visiting places like **Liz's Antique Hardware**, with its well-loved doorknobs and perfectly well-worn trims. Even if your SoCal home is filled with shiny and modern things, **Liz's** will help you inject it with a bit of brassy patina and vintage glamour.

mister freedom

vintage clothing, shoes and accessories

7161 Beverly Boulevard
Between Formosa and Detroit
(Mid-City) *map S24*
323.653.2014
www.misterfreedom.com

twitter @_misterfreedom_
daily noon - 7p

Yes, Please: *mister freedom originals: le paletot apache, pantalon peau de diable, american sportswear collection, selvedge denim, indigo dyed henleys; vintage clothing*

I often feel like there are fewer than six degrees of separation between the businesses that appear in these books. In this case, it was three degrees: **Lost & Found** pointed me to **Bazar**, where I was then aimed to **Mister Freedom**. It's like playing connect the dots. **Mister Freedom** is like finding yourself on the set of M*A*S*H*. Half of the space isfilled with vintage army boots, jeans, tees, and military memorabilia. The other half is all about the in-house line of clothing for men and Japanese selvedge denim. Since I'm feeling pretty good at this three degrees of separation game, I'm now going to try to connect Kevin Bacon and Alan Alda in less than six steps.

rolling greens

home store and nursery with vintage flair

7505 Beverly Boulevard
Corner of North Gardner
(Mid-City) *map S25*
323.934.4500
www.rollinggreensnursery.com

twitter @rollinggreensla
mon - sat 10a - 6p sun 11a - 6p
event floral design.
flower arranging workshops

Yes, Please: *hornet's nests and beehives from texas, fresh hand tied flower bouquets, k. hall room diffusers, libeco linens, vintage birdcages, fresh herb plants*

Whatever part of your home needs a pick me up, a bit of inspiration or simply some good old fashioned retail therapy, Rolling Greens has the solution. Is your green thumb itching? Browse the nursery for herbs and plants, or take a free of charge "edible garden" workshop. Does your bathroom feel drab? Pick up some linen hand towels or vintage light fixtures. Bored with your go-to dinners? Re-energize your inner Mario with a large selection of cookbooks from around the world. **Rolling Greens** has something for every mood, every room, and everyone.

mid-city west

west hollywood

eat

shop

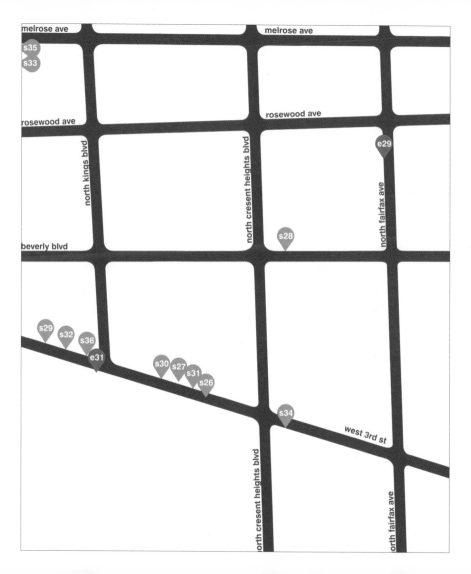

animal

like nothing else in los angeles

435 North Fairfax Avenue
Between Rosewood and Oakwood
(Mid-City West) *map E29*
323.782.9225
www.animalrestaurant.com

sun - thu 6 - 11p fri - sat 6p - 1a
dinner
$$. reservations recommended

Yes, Please: *06 baxter henneberg vineyard pinot noir;
little yella pils; pig ear, chili, lime, fried egg; barbeque pork
belly sandwiches; sticky toffee pudding, mascarpone, orange*

Right around the time I was first heading to Animal, I was on the fence of vegetarianism, checking out the greener grass on the other side of the pig pen. If there is anywhere that has me hopping back in the pen, it's **Animal**. Crisp pig ear with chili and lime! Sweetbreads and creamed spinach! Ribs and rabbit, foie gras and oxtail. Eating here is a brilliant study on how delicious the animal can be, from head to tail. And if you would prefer not to eat animals, one of my favorite delights here is the delicious gnocchi. Regardless of which side of the fence you sit on, **Animal** is the place to be.

df feet

unique men's shoes

8304 West Third Street
Between Sweetzer and Flores
(Mid-City West) *map S26*
323.651.5014

mon - sat 10a - 6p sun noon - 5p

Yes. Please: *george esquivel/fratelli rossetti collaboration, florsheim by duckie brown saddle shoes, martin margiela boots, belstaff, billykirk bags, happy socks, falke socks*

My sister and I have owned a men's clothing store for ten years, and we've become pretty good at revamping men's entire wardrobes. One problem with these newly well-dressed men: they are not always well-heeled. One of the questions asked of us over the years over and over again is "where should I go to buy shoes?" **DF Feet** is the answer. With an incredibly unique selection of shoes from around the world, they have everything a dapper man might need including local California designer and cobbler George Esquivel's beautiful shoes. I say that **DF Feet** is a must stop for any man with sartorial instincts.

eggy

beautiful children's apparel with heavy french and japanese influence

8365 West 3rd Street
Corner of Kings Road
(Mid-City West) *map S27*
323.658.8882
www.shopeggy.com

mon - fri 10:30a - 6:30p
sat 11a - 6p sun noon-5p
online shopping

Yes, Please: *kit + lili cotton romper, makie anything, eco playdough, bensimon sneakers, tane organics kimono style onesie, tegu blocks, little nest, sirrmax push car*

Eggy stands out from other children's clothing stores for one main reason: I really want the tiny items made in my size! If the linen dresses and beautiful cotton tunics seem perfect for me, then I doubly want them for my soon to be born baby. **Eggy's** owner buys much of the adorable goods here from Japan and France, countries that are arbiters of style and design. A bonus that happened while at **Eggy** was that the manager Monika, also an astrologist, gave me some insight into my little girl's future personality! Some much needed words for any anxious mother to be!

eveleigh

surprising gem on the sunset strip

**8752 Sunset Boulevard
Corner of Sherbourne
(West Hollywood)** *map E30*
**424.239.1630
www.theeveleigh.com**

twitter @theeveleigh
see website for hours
brunch. lunch. dinner
$$ reservations recommended

Yes, Please: *housemade gin and tonic; bubble & squeak, chicken schnitzel sandwich with sweet pickles, quinoa salad, roasted bone marrow, wild white shrimp, peach crumble*

Here's the tricky thing about eating in L.A. We've got the ethnic food, food carts and serious hole-in-the wall eateries covered, but sometimes you want a pretty place to eat with a little ambience and some great vibes. And I'm not talking about the 'vibes' offered at most celebrity-owned, sceney, mediocre-at-best food, over-designed places. Not to be a total girl, but I want a place where I would want to wear heels, flirt with the bartender and still eat and drink deliciously. **Eveleigh** (pronounced Everly), with its beautiful, romantic room overlooking the city, delivers on all accounts. This is what I'm talking about!

inheritance

antique, vintage and artful housewares

8055 Beverly Boulevard
Between Crescent Heights and Laurel
(Mid-City West) *map S28*
323.658.6756
www.inheritanceshop.com

mon - fri 11a - 6p sat 11a - 5p
sun by appointment only
online shopping

Yes, Please: *rs barcelona football table, vintage booze bottles, the new english anatomica espresso cup & saucer, vintage corkscrews, reichenbach peace soliders*

Though I personally love a clean design aesthetic when it comes to home décor, I secretly admire homes where the owner has the flair to mix the slightly offbeat and obscure with more expected pieces. So when I walked through **Inheritance** (formerly **Zelen**), my secret admiration grew and grew. Mike's got the knack for this look, and suddenly I wanted to throw out my whole clean and minimal thing and start over. But short of buying this entire store and installing it directly in my house, which sounds highly appealing, it might not be cost-effective at this moment. I'll just get a piece or two here, and start there.

new stone age

glorious gifts

8407 West Third Street
Between Croft and Orlando
(Mid-City West) *map S29*
323.658.5969
www.newstoneagela.com

mon - sat 11a - 6p sun noon - 5p

Yes, Please: *letter balls, a veritable emporium of jewelry!, bird whistles, ceramic keys, vintage metallic thread, emporium glass glitter*

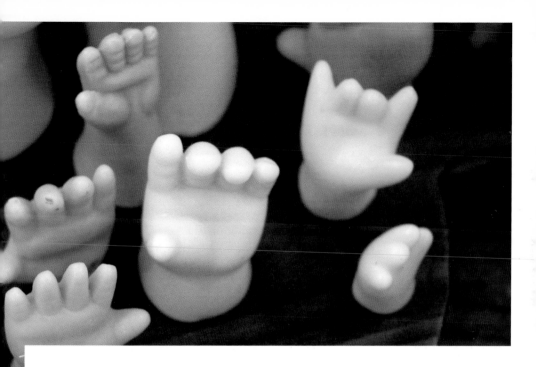

My family members are competitive gift givers. Over the years it's almost developed into an extreme sport (maybe ESPN will devote a show to it). It's all about who finds the most unique things, who wraps the most creatively, who follows a theme the best. So come birthdays and holidays, the pressure is on. With **New Stone Age** as my secret weapon, I'm now as calm as the proverbial cucumber. Just about everything in this store is bound to impress my picky clan, and I'm pretty certain that these treasures are going to help win me the gold medal of gift giving.

noodle stories

fashion-forward women's store

8323 West Third Street
Between Flores and Sweetzer
(Mid-City West) *map S30*
323.651.1782
www.noodlestories.com

mon - sat 10a - 6p sun noon - 5p

Yes, Please: *viktor & rolf, tao, martin margiela,*
junya watanabe, comme des garçons, antipast, y's by yohji
yamamoto, issey miyake, hache

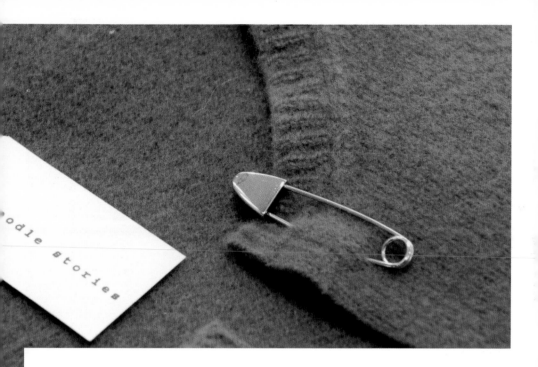

Who is it that came up with the rules for dressing, and why do we blindly follow ones like the silly "No white linen after Labor Day"? Who knows. So thank goodness there's a place like **Noodle Stories**—where they celebrate breaking the rules and being fashion nonconformists. This is where you can find shoes that don't necessarily match perfectly and clothes that playfully disregard symmetry. If having fun with fashion and being an individualist appeals to your sharp and savvy noodle, then **Noodle Stories** is the place for you.

ok

home goods and personal accessories

**8303 West Third Street
Corner of Sweetzer
(Mid-City West)** *map S31*
**323.653.3501
www.okthestore.com**

mon - sat 11a - 6:30p sun noon - 6p
online shopping. registries

Yes. Please: *heath ceramics, noguchi lamp, vintage phones, riedel glassware, anne ricketts bronze sculptures, enzo mari perpetual calendar, gio ponti flatware, pippa small jewelry*

You will find that a lot of modern lifestyle stores (also called urban tchotchke stores) stock a large selection of silly fluff—i.e., goofily designed objects with no useful purpose other than to clutter up one's life. OK is not one of said stores. You will find absolutely no fluff here. This is a shopping environment where every item has a purpose. Each of these carefully chosen objects is well vetted by the knowledgeable and no-nonsense Larry, who has a sharp eye for finding the quality goods you want in your home. Fun, ok. Fluff, not ok.

plastica

colorful, functional objects

8405 West Third Street
Between Orlando and Croft
(Mid-City West) *map S32*
323.655.1051
www.plasticashop.com

mon - sat 11a - 6p sun noon - 5p
online shopping

Yes, Please: *bento boxes, modkat litter box, whitelines perfect bound notebook, lamy safari pen & pencil, france matchbook postcards, rody, chilewich ombre shag mats*

I have one word for you: Plastica. Maybe if this had been the advice given to young Benjamin Braddock at his graduation party, he might not have gotten seduced by Mrs. Robinson. No doubt this store could lure in anyone, old and young alike, curing those who think shopping is boring. I know this is a big claim for a simple store, but check out **Plastica's** punchy-colored array of playfully functional, internationally-sourced items and you'll agree. Remember, when giving useful tips, **Plastica** should be at the top of your list.

rth
handcrafted leather accessories

537 North La Cienega Boulevard
Corner of Melrose Avenue
(Mid-City West) *map S33*
310.289.7911
www.rthshop.com

tue - sat 11a - 6:30p

Yes, Please: *leather feather pins, belts and wristbands, vintage beaded buckles, beaded friendship bracelets, leather envelopes & clutches, vintage linen nightgown*

Upon entering RTH, your senses are immediately stimulated. The strong smell of freshly cut leather fills your nose and you want to touch everything in sight. The environment here evokes the feel of the open range, and even more so when owner Rene Holguin shares his family's story, which includes learning the leather working craft from his father, a bootmaker in El Paso, Texas. Rene has honed these skills over the years and applies them to not only traditional leather pieces but also modern items such as iPod cases. Rene mixes his handcrafted **RTH** designs with some pitch perfect vintage pieces making the overall experience feel all the more authentic.

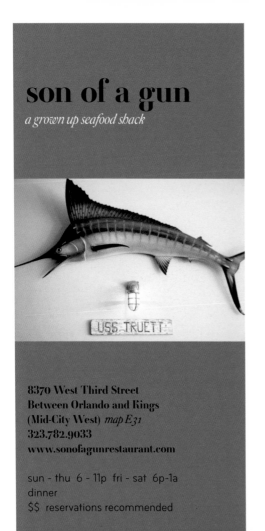

son of a gun

a grown up seafood shack

8370 West Third Street
Between Orlando and Kings
(Mid-City West) *map E31*
323.782.9033
www.sonofagunrestaurant.com

sun - thu 6 - 11p fri - sat 6p-1a
dinner
$$ reservations recommended

Yes, Please: *aviation cocktail, lobster roll with celery &
lemon aioli, king crab leg with tabasco butter, frozen lime
yogurt with graham crumble & toasted meringue*

"This reminds me of the Oregon coast," I remarked. "Really? I think it feels like Lake Michigan," spoke Amy. Then, Jon, the owner, shared, "It's Florida for me." And that's the whole point. **Son of a Gun** is a nostalgic hybrid of everybody's summer memories of sandcastles, boating and shucking oysters. East Coasters will rejoice with the lobster roll while us Westerners can delight in crab and spot prawns. No matter where you're from, you'll be taken back to another place... especially when indulging in the festive, umbrella-garnished cocktails.

south willard

a soothing, smart men's store

8038 West Third Street
Between Crescent Heights and Edinburgh
(Mid-City West) *map S34*
323.653.6153
www.southwillard.com

mon - sat noon - 6p sun noon - 5p
online shopping

Yes, Please: *vibram sandals for south willard, stephan schneider, mhl. shirts, dries van noten, band of outsiders ties, postal co. card cases*

Do you find these days that being calm is a bit tough? Most people I know are having to double-up on the Bikram yoga to help keep the stress at bay. I have a different method, which is to visit **South Willard**. Neutral and primary colored men's clothing and accessories is the story here, with everything carefully hung, placed and stacked in moderation—with attention to straight lines and even spacing. Ahhh, I'm soothed just thinking about it. Men, if you don't want thumping music blasting away while you shop or duuuuuudes helping you find your wardrobe, this is your spot.

tenoversix

forward-thinking style

8425 Melrose Avenue
Between Melrose Place and La Cienega
(Mid-City West) *map S35*
323.330.9355
www.tenover6.com

twitter @tenoversix
mon - sat 11a - 6p
online shopping

Yes, Please: *tenoversix, acne pop, lizzie fortunato jewels, wren, manimal, filippa k, dieppa restrepo, david ash, six scents, bobo choses*

"Ten over six" translates to ten shillings, sixpence—the price of the Mad Hatter's hat in *Alice in Wonderland*. Though you won't find anything for this lowly pittance in **Tenoversix**, you will absolutely find a collection of things as quirky and cool as that nutter, the Mad Hatter. And though there is no riddle here to solve, it's crystal clear that this store is full of amazing things to wear and carry. The only thing that dismayed me at **Tenoversix** was that there were so many things I wanted, my head was spinning like I'd just been on MH's teacup ride.

traveler's bookcase

a great little travel book shop

8375 West Third Street
Between Orlando and Kings
(Mid-City West) *map S36*
323.655.0575
www.travelersbookcase.com

twitter @travelersbooks
see website for hours
online shopping

Yes, Please: *guides: luxe, city walks, le cool; maps, maps, maps, "this is rome" by miroslav sasek, "the good girl's guide to getting lost" by rachel friedman, moleskin anything*

"Brilliant and seductive."
—*People* (four stars)

TRESPASS

My husband Shawn is a voracious traveler. Every time he goes to a new place, he buys three guidebooks and two maps. I've even had to enact a rule that a plane ticket must be bought before a guidebook can be. But when I entered **Traveler's Bookcase**, the rules changed. In fact, if I would have had my suitcase with me, I could have had it filled in a minute flat—clothing and personal effects would have been jettisoned to make room for one of the best collections of guidebooks, maps and travel-related fiction I've ever seen. So Shawn, where are we going? Because I've got the guide for it.

venice

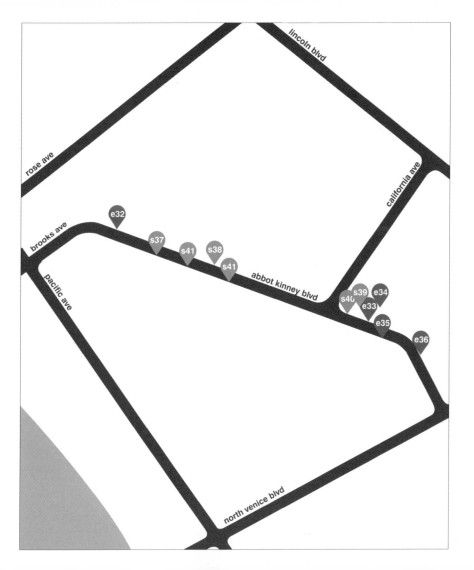

axe

classic california cuisine

1009 Abbot Kinney Boulevard
Between Brooks and Broadway
(Venice) *map E32*
310.664.9787
www.axerestaurant.com

see website for hours
brunch. lunch. dinner
$$ reservations accepted

Yes, Please: *anderson valley pale ale, fresh mint drink, composed salad plate, grilled hooks white cheddar sandwich, spicy chicken soup, chocolate brownie pudding*

In this spread-out city, people stick to their side of town. You know, birds of a feather flock together. If you live in Venice, you rarely travel to Silver Lake. If Highland Park is home, you probably don't spend a lot of time in Brentwood. There is a flock, though, who will go anywhere and everywhere. This group is made up of the **Axe** bird. They might live on the east side or downtown, but **Axe** in Venice is still their favorite restaurant in town. Even after a fire closed the place down for a year, this intensely loyal migratory flock returned in droves. **Axe** is that good.

bazar

unusual finds, old and new

1108c Abbot Kinney Boulevard
Between Westminster and San Juan
(Venice) *map S37*
310.314.2101

wed - sat noon - 6p sun noon - 5p

Yes, Please: *vintage linens, mister freedom denim,*
japanese street signs, felt rocks, woven bags, antique boards
with arabic script, vintage furniture

Here are some definitions for a bazaar. 1. A market consisting of a street lined with shops and stalls, especially in the Orient or Middle East. 2. A shop in which miscellaneous articles are sold. 3. An outstanding place in Venice that encompasses the first two meanings of the word. Though this modern **Bazar** is tucked on the Abbot Kinney strip, you could imagine once inside that you were far, far away from Southern California. And like the busy souks of Morocco or Cairo, this street on a weekend demands some respite, which you can find inside the calmness of this intriguing spot.

bountiful

pretty things for a pretty home

1335 Abbot Kinney Boulevard
Between Santa Clara and California
(Venice) *map S38*
310.450.3620
www.bountifulhome.com

daily 10:30a - 7p

Yes, Please: *shells, shells & more shells!, cake stand collection, alabaster lamps, chandeliers, vintage armoires, côté bastide bath products*

I used to go to Florida every year for spring break with my family. We stayed at my grandparents' place, where we would spend hours on the white beach looking for seashells. My grandmother had an incredible eye; she could find the rarest, most beautiful shells, and her collection was exquisite. The big bins of shells at **Bountiful** make me think of her and her finds. While I will never have her skill in seeking, and my trips to Florida have become rare, I can always come to this sun-bleached shop and fill bags of seashells to take home with me, in case I need a bit of the sea and Gammy's memory.

gjelina

rustic american food that draws crowds

1429 Abbot Kinney Boulevard
Corner of Milwood (Venice) *map E33*
310.450.1429
www.gjelina.com

mon - fri 11:30a - midnight
sat - sun 9a - midnight brunch until 3p
brunch. lunch. dinner
$$ reservations recommended

Yes, Please: *the visionary cocktail; duck liver & pork shoulder pâté; farro, squash & kale soup; guanciale, green olive, fresno chile & buffalo mozzarella pizza*

Gjelina is a beautiful restaurant. Though a gorgeous girl might be one in a million in this city, a beautiful restaurant here is a bird of a different feather. From the etched wall carvings to the vintage wood and metal school chairs, to the rough-hewn center table and the quirky lightbulb chandelier, to big bowls filled with orange tomatoes and figs. But **Gjelina** is more than just a pretty face; the food is substantial and prepared with precision. Smart, pretty and delicious. I think **Gjelina** might be lust at first sight, love at first taste.

gta
gjelina takey away

1427 Abbot Kinney Boulevard
Corner of Milwood
(Venice) *map E34*
310.392.7575
www.gjelina.com

daily 7a - 9p
breakfast. lunch. treats
$-$$ first come, first served

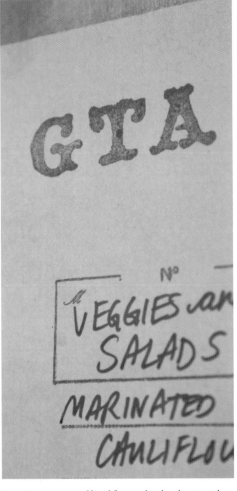

Yes. Please: *assorted breakfast sandwiches, biscuit with butter and rhubarb jam, panzanella with burrata, pork meatball sandwich, bitter greens and bacon, carrot cake*

The fact that my husband is very thin is only frustrating when he devours copious amounts of baked goods. Normally self-restrained by healthy eating habits, he behaves like an addict, unsure of when he will receive his next fix, in the face of a good scone. **GTA** (stands for **Gjelina Take Away**) had such an effect on him one morning that I think he spoiled his dinner as well as his breakfast the next day. His baked good demons popped up as I watched him order a scone with butter and apricot jam, carrot cake, and then a blueberry muffin. I looked away for a moment, and when I turned to leave, David had three to go bags in hand. **GTA** is that addictive.

linus bikes

modern classic city bikes

1413 1/2 Abbot Kinney Boulevard
Between California and Milwood
(Venice) *map S39*
310.857.7777
www.linusbike.com

twitter @linusbike
mon - wed 11a - 6p thu - sun 11a - 7p

Yes, Please: *bikes: roadster classic, roadster sport, dutchi, mixte, baskets, bags*

I probably walked by the attractive, shiny bikes lined up along Abbot Kinney in front of **Milkmade** maybe five or six times before I realized that they were part of an outdoor showroom of sorts for the locally made **Linus Bikes**. Walk down the alley and there you'll find a small store where you can further admire an array of bikes, smartly designed bike bags and accessories and get a chance to meet the owners and bikemakers. I've been on the lookout for a classic city bike for a couple of years now, and a cream colored **Linus** bike with all the accoutrements is now at the top of my wish list.

milkmade

stylish shop for guys and girls

1413 Abbot Kinney Boulevard
Between California and Milwood
(Venice) *map S40*
310.581.8890
www.shop.milkmade.eu

twitter @milkmade1413
tue - sat 11a - 7p sun noon - 6p
online shopping

Yes, Please: *low classic, harvey faircloth, hoss jewelry, garbstore, momotaro jeans by japan blue, sunny sports, the green soccer journal, le labo candles*

It's generally a good thing that my growing belly has forced some restraint when it comes to shopping while I'm working on these books. But when I entered **Milkmade**, I was immediately bummed about the limitations brought on by my quickly expanding baby girth, i.e., a stretchy waistband is imperative. This is a store of beautifully tailored clothing with intricate details that show off a figure—clothing that is quite the opposite of the shapeless tents I'm wearing right now. Ahhh **Milkmade**, I will return to you. Just as soon as I'm out of my pull-up pants.

shima

heart-healthy sushi

1432 Abbot Kinney Boulevard
Between Navarre and Palms
(Venice) *map E35*
310.314.0882

tue - sat 5:30 - 10:30p
dinner
$$-$$$ reservations accepted

Yes, Please: *nigori with pomegranate, brown rice green tea, organic homemade tofu, kelp shooter, japanese aji spanish mackerel sashimi, baby halibut sashimi*

Not that it was ever a consideration, but doing this book without featuring a great sushi place would be like doing the Chicago book without a pizza place. Is it a problem to find a fantastic sushi place in this town? No, as there are a number of them (**Kiyokawa**, for example). But is there a place that's a true original? Yes: **Shima**. Aside from offering top-notch fish, the focus here is on being as healthful as possible, using brown rice, divine housemade tofu and no non-fish animal fats. This creates a menu that is as good for you as it is good to eat and is quintessentially L.A.

the tasting kitchen

seasonal, northwest-inspired food

mardi 8 septembre

« A Gammon of bacon you shall recei
And bear it hence with love and good
For this is our custom at Dunmow well
Though the sport be ours, the bacon's
— London ca. 17

1633 Abbot Kinney Boulevard
Between Venice and Palms
(Venice) *map E36*
310.392.6644
www.thetastingkitchen.com

twitter @ttkvenice
dinner daily 6p - close
brunch sat - sun 10:30a - 2p
$$-$$$ reservations accepted

Yes, Please: *angelico cocktail, wings with apple cider &
flax seed, endive; cara cara & medjool dates salad, cod
with black rice & satsuma*

Portland, Oregon, where I grew up, seems to be the city du jour these days, especially for foodies and young creative types. But it's not all wine and roses there, and some—like the entire kitchen crew at **The Tasting Kitchen**— have moved to smoggier pastures. My sister and I hung with Bartender Justin—another Portland expat—at the bar and shared P-town stories while watching him craft an array of bitters. Rumor has it that this place came together in six days, but once you taste Chef Casey's food, you won't care if it's been open six hours or six years. It's just plain good.

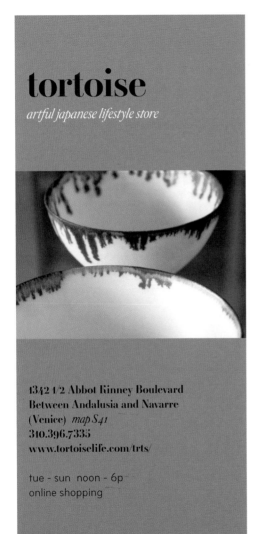

tortoise

artful japanese lifestyle store

1342 1/2 Abbot Kinney Boulevard
Between Andalusia and Navarre
(Venice) *map S41*
310.396.7335
www.tortoiselife.com/trts/

tue - sun noon - 6p
online shopping

3**KG**

Yes, Please: *ryota aoki pitcher & katakuchi, string & button close envelope, marc newson cutlery, shigeki fujishiro stool, shoji morinaga wooden bowl, yasuki hiramatsu rings*

Though these days urban clothes horses think of the term "slow and steady wins the race" as a groovy clothing line, I think of the saying in conjunction with **Tortoise**. We modern folk often feel rushed to decorate and fill our homes, getting items cheaply and quickly instead of searching for things that will last longer but might take more time to source. For those steady sorts of collectors, **Tortoise** is a mecca. Everything in this little store emphasizes quality over quantity and will remind you that patience, not speed, will serve you best in the end.

tortoise general store

general store for japanese goods

**1208 Abbott Kinney Boulevard
Between San Juan and Santa Clara
(Venice)** *map S42*
**310.314.8448
www.tortoisegeneralstore.com**

tue - sat 11:30a - 6:30p sun noon - 6p
online shopping

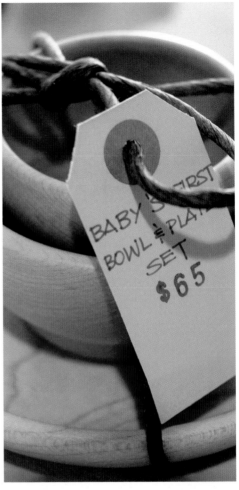

Yes, Please: *kaikado canisters, straw trivet, mari balls tenugui traditional fabrics, hario ceramic dripper, yanagi flatware, stone handle bags, colored paper tape,*

Okay, everything I just said in Tortoise's blurb about being patient and about taking your time with your home and what you fill it with? Yeah, well, scratch that for a moment and come to **Tortoise General Store** and STOCK UP!! I kid you not. Hurry, because things here don't stick around for long. Taku and Keiko are constantly filling their mini-emporium with must-have-now pieces sourced from Japan and beyond. I think they should have named this sister spot to **Tortoise** The Hare—but I will keep my nose out of naming and let my fingers do the buying.

santa monica

brentwood

shop

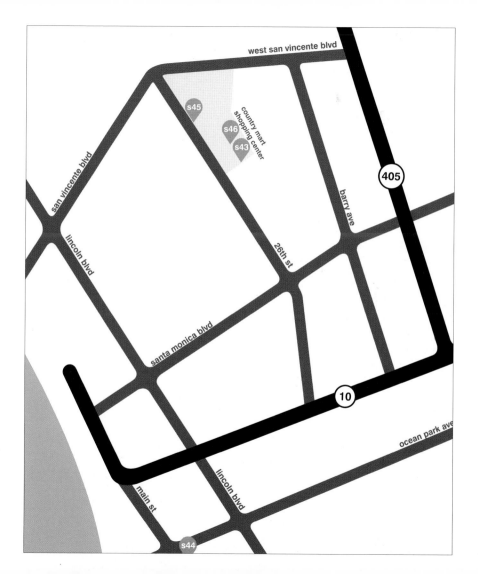

botany
desirable florals

225 26th Street
In the Brentwood Country Mart
(Brentwood) *map S43*
310.394.0358
www.botanyflowers.com

twitter @botanyflowers
mon - sat 10a - 6p sun 11a - 5p
custom orders. design. events

Yes, Please: *gorgeous arrangements, cut flowers, succulents, terrariums, citrus trees, beekman 1802 soaps, haws watering can, d. landreth seeds*

I see the email from Anna; it seems urgent. It goes something like this: "There's a new florist that's just opened in the Country Mart. You NEED to go check it out." And so I hopped in my rented Dodge Caravan and careened down PCH to **Botany** (12 minutes from Malibu to Brentwood, not bad!). And yes Anna, your sources had it right. **Botany** is gorgeous. My first sight of this little space at the back of the Mart was of a black wall that seemed to be sprouting flowers. Smile. And then talking to the effervescent co-owner Stacie Rubaum made me want to have her fill my world with blooms.

When her son complained of being bored, Mad Men's Betty Draper retorted, "Boring people are bored; go bang your head against a wall." My real-world advice for those afflicted with ennui? Boring people are bored; go to **Obsolete**. It's not possible for boredom to exist here. The moment you set foot into this amazing place, you'll feel as though you've entered another realm of the universe. Though many of the eclectic array of objects may have come from obsolete eras, new life has come to them when co-mingled with modern, slightly macabre artwork. This **Obsolete** is the antithesis of over.

post 26

stylish shop for women

225 26th Street
In the Brentwood Country Mart
(Brentwood) *map S45*
310.451.0950
www.posttwentysix.com

mon - sat 10a - 6p sun noon - 4p

Yes, Please: *alexander wang, 3.1 phillip lim, anna sui, rick owens lilies, see by chloe, anya hindmarch, k jacques shoes, pare gabia shoes, 88 by bing bang, landver*

Jeannine Braden is someone's best friend. I'm insanely jealous of whoever this person is, because Jeannine is the best friend we all want: fashionable, witty and able to think outside the box—just like her store **Post 26**. This place is packed, and I mean PACKED, with vintage shoes, new designs, old designs, refurbished jewelry, etc. You want her as a best friend to lend you a pair of shoes for a first date or to have that last perfect accessory on the day of your wedding. You'll want her for every style crisis and celebration. For now, just shop at her store. It's the next best thing to having Jeannine as your best friend.

sugar paper

custom letterpress studio and paper goods shop

225 26th Street, #27
In the Brentwood Country Mart
(Brentwood) *map S46*
1749 Ensley Avenue (Century City)
Between Eastborne and Santa Monica
sm 310.451.7870 / cc 310.277.7804
www.sugarpaper.com

twitter @sugarpaperla
mon - fri 10a - 6p sat 10a - 5p sun 11a - 5p
online shopping. custom orders

Yes, Please: *sugar paper: custom letterpress, audrey desk calendar, recipe box, alphabet coasters, market list; oh joy note pads, hammerpress calendars, linneas lights*

Yes, Virginia, there are people who still write letters. Take, for example, my friend Katie, who writes such eloquent thank you notes, I'm tempted to frame them. My thank yous pale in comparison with Katie's, but I do love to send and receive beautiful cards, and one of the best places to find gorgeous goods is at **Sugar Paper**. From custom letterpress to their own prettier-than-pretty line of paper goods to a carefully picked assortment of other letterpressed delights—the message you send on something from here will be memorable, whether you're able to express it in words or by your choice of card.

finito

happy travels to you

rather *los angeles*

isbn-13 9780984425389

copyright 2011 ©swiftrank. printed in the usa

every effort has been made to ensure the accuracy of the information in this book. however, certain details are subject to change. please remember when using the guides that hours alter seasonally and sometimes sadly, businesses close. the publisher cannot accept responsibility for any consequences arising from the use of this book.

editing / fact checking + production: chloe fields
in design master: nicole conant
map design + production: julia dickey + bryan wolf

thx' to our friends at designers & agents for their hospitality and their support of the rather experience. please visit > designersandagents.com

rather is distributed by
independent publishers group > www.ipgbook.com

to peer further into the world of **rather** and to buy books, please visit **rather.com** to learn more